CATS ARE FROM SATURN

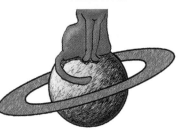

DOGS ARE FROM PLUTO

BY RON ROBINSON
WITH ILLUSTRATIONS
BY THE AUTHOR

EX MACHINA PUBLISHING COMPANY

CATS ARE FROM SATURN / DOGS ARE FROM PLUTO, by Ron Robinson, with illustrations by the author.

First Edition
First Printing August 1998

Ex Machina Publishing Company
Box 448
Sioux Falls, SD 57101

Library of Congress Catalog Number: 98-92430

ISBN 0-944287-20--4 (Softbound)
ISBN 0-944287-21-2 (Hardbound)

Dedicated
to Lady I, Lady II, Indy, Janis, Maisie,
Cutie, Midge, Dan, Ike, Pooch, Binkie,
and all the other dogs and cats
we've known and loved.

Cat Levitating

CATS ARE FROM SATURN, DOGS ARE FROM PLUTO

A family is a unit composed not only of children but of men, women, an occasional animal, and the common cold.
— *Ogden Nash*

It must be raining cats and dogs. I just stepped in a poodle.
— *Red Skelton*

For centuries it was believed that, since dogs and cats appeared to be mammals, they shared a common ancestor in the evolutionary chain. Assuming there is something to the theory of evolution, that would mean there once existed on earth a creature, call it a "dat" or a "cog," that ate tuna, slept all day, wagged its tail, panted, purred, chased itself, and wouldn't come when called.

Scientists have produced not a single fossil with these characteristics, although in the 19th century P.T. Barnum exhibited the bones of a creature he called "The Missing Lynx,"which appeared to have the head of a dog, the tail of a cat, and the body of a large rabbit, and which he claimed to have been found in a gravel pit in Iowa. The whole thing turned out to be a hoax fabricated by schoolboys, but that did not prevent Barnum from continuing to profit from the exhibit, billing it "The Outrageous Darwinian Deceit."

What should have been obvious to even the casual observer, and most especially to those who had actual experience as "owners" of dogs or cats or dogs AND cats, was that they were not merely different species, but different lifeforms entirely.

SATURNIANS

When I play with my cat, who knows whether she is not amusing herself with me more than I with her.
— *Michel de Montaigne*

Cats are from Saturn. Their cells are not carbon-based, as are the cells of most living organisms on Earth, but silicon-based, which means that while they may appear graceful and fragile as a glass decanter, they are actually as tough and resilient as a fiberglass rowboat. The silicon nature of the animal may be detected as well in its glassy eyes, which are capable of staring down any carbon-based organism, from an amoeba on up.

Its nature is betrayed as well in a cat's fondness for computers, which are likewise silicon-based beings. While the dog is a Luddite who prefers the technology of the Stone Age (or as dogs call it, the Bone Age), a cat will often be found napping comfortably on or about a desktop computer, which it regards as the closest approximation to catdom to be found on Earth.

Like a cat, the computer sits there all day purring, not doing what it is told, and when not in use, nodding off. From time to time, a cat may even undertake some paws-on net surfing, although it prefers to bat the mouse around rather than use the keyboard. One is best advised to avoid cat chatrooms, however; the din is deafening.

The gravity of Saturn, a thousand times that of Earth, owing to its enormous mass, gave cats the apparent ability to levitate. The average housecat would weigh literally a ton on Saturn, and would crawl about the landscape like an alligator, dragging its body through the Saturnian slime.

When they migrated to Earth to escape the population explosion, cats discovered they could fly. Not literally, of course, since being neither avian nor angelic, they had no wings; but the energy which on Saturn would slide them a few centimeters (rather than inches, Saturn being on the metric system), on Earth would propel them several feet (rather than meters, Earth being on the system in which everything is measured by the length of a basketball player's sneaker).

Like Superman (who was of course from Krypton, which was almost as massive as Saturn) they found they could "leap tall buildings in a single bound" as long as the building wasn't too tall and they got a running start. From a standing start they could levitate to table-height with the slightest shove.

There is some question whether they can remain suspended in air any length of time. A Persian kitten was once observed to float for two minutes and 32 seconds, but you know how the Persians exaggerate. The average cat can remain airborne for probably no longer than 45 seconds, and then only if badly startled.

Try breaking in on your cat while it is sleeping soundly, which could be any time during the day, or when it is performing its ritual ablutions, at which time it appears to have discovered a fascinating bon-bon under its thigh, and you can test your own cat's staying power. It helps if you bark loudly.

The American record for mid-air suspension is one minute and ten seconds, held by Buffy of Oshkosh, Wisconsin. (Foreign judges cry foul, however, claiming that the cat was not really floating but rather clinging to the ceiling, having been badly startled by a pit bull.)

PLUTONIANS

> If you pick up a starving dog and make him prosperous, he will not bite you. This is the principal difference between a dog and a man.
> — *Mark Twain*

Dogs are from Pluto, which as any schoolboy knows is the planet at the outermost fringe of the solar system and therefore the last to be discovered, being added to the skycharts by Walt Disney in 1932 and named after a cartoon character. (Having discovered Pluto, Disney went on to discover Goofy, a dog who could talk and who wore working clothes with a vest and a silly hat, but who was still as dumb as... well, as a dog.)

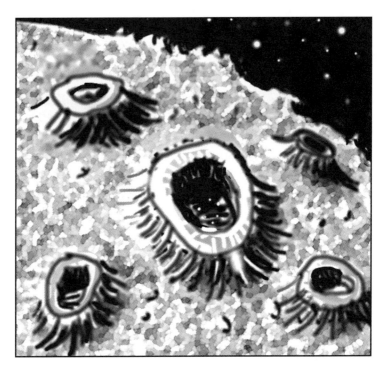

Recent orbital photographs from the surface of
Pluto reveal craters in the shape of toilet bowls,
believed by NASA scientists to be ancient water-
ing holes.

Pluto is a dumb planet, and most dogs, as a
consequence are dumb, or at least dumb by cat
standards. Unlike cats, who migrated to Earth
with a definite purpose, *i.e.*, to overpopulate it
with their offspring, dogs simply broke the
chain and wandered away. Some were put in a
pound on Jupiter, where they are still waiting to
be claimed, while others strayed to Earth where
they became companions to men, who are not

Before the Dawn of Civilization

so bright either, again according to cat standards.

Dogs seemed especially attracted to the male of the human species, recognizing him as somehow kindred. A man's best friend, it is said, is a dog, while a woman's best friend is a box of chocolate.

The Dawn of Civilization

Together, man and dog hunted, fished, drank beer, told lies, burped, and exclaimed, "It doesn't get any better than this." Woman, meanwhile stayed home with her kitties, had babies, cooked, cleaned, made beds, and said, "It damn well better get better than this." Then woman invented civilization, and neither man nor dog has had a moment's rest since, while women and cats have increasingly improved their lot.

A dog cannot fly, at least not to his knowledge. One explanation for the dog's inability to get off the ground is that it is, naturally enough, a plutonium-based life form, and plutonium is by definition a heavy metal. It can irradiate, it can explode, but it can't fly.

Still, some objective observers believe that a dog's inability to fly is purely psychological. Occasionally, having treed a squirrel, a dog wishes it could fly, or climb, or something, but its levitation ability remains untested, even though theoretically, judging from Pluto's mass, transplanted Plutonians should be able to float as easily as Tabby.

The truth of the matter, it seems increasingly clear, is that dogs are afraid of flying. They have seen it, and it doesn't look safe to them. How do cats do that? they wonder. And why? And how do cats always land on their feet?

They have watched younger males of the human species drop cats from rooftops to test the feline ability to dislocate their spines in midair, rotate half their torsos at a time, and land on all fours. The canine response has been to run and hide under the porch, lest the young males of the human species look around for further subjects of experimentation.

Dogs know they can't rotate their spines like that. They have experienced relatively small leaps which have resulted in spectacular and painful pratfalls, after which they pick themselves up, wag their tails, and act nonchalant. If God had wanted them to fly, they believe, He

Young human males conduct scientific investigation into Saturnian landing patterns.

would have given them rotating spines and a sense of balance, like a cat's. They steadfastly refuse to take the leap, and remain earthbound. Cats, of course, attribute this flightlessness to a lack of imagination.

Dog Paddle . . . . . .Cat Walk

Dogs can swim, of course, which partially makes up for their inability to levitate. Dogs learned to swim when their masters attempted to drown them. Cats, who come from a planet devoid of H2O, detest water for any purpose, be it drinking, bathing, or swimming. For drinking, cats prefer champagne; for bathing, a good scrub with their own tongues; for swimming, walking on water, or at least attempting to do so.

COMMUNICATION BETWEEN CATS AND DOGS

Animals talk to each other, of course.
There can be no question about that; but I
suppose there are very few people who can
understand them.
— Mark Twain

Strictly speaking, there is no communication between cats and dogs, unless war is considered a means of communication. They simply do not speak the same language, and they steadfastly refuse to try. Like Americans in a foreign country, they believe that it will suffice merely to speak louder. When a dog attempts politely to tell a cat to remove its face from the dog's food dish, then is forced to repeat itself less politely and at greater volume, all to no avail, there seems no recourse but to violence.

The same is true of a cat, except for the polite part. The cat will yowl once or twice, then slap the dog in the face, its claws fully extended. Or it may omit the yowling altogether and simply unsheathe its nails immediately.

Dogs occasionally rely upon the surprise factor, knowing that a cat's delicate nervous system will betray it into running when caught off guard. The chase will last until the cat regains its accustomed composure, takes a stand, and opens its mouth in what in cat language is a ma-

Plain Plutonian: "That guy is stealing our garbage again!"

jor expletive, which sounds something like this: "CAAAAHTT!"

The dog is always surprised by that, loses its balance in attempting to backpedal, and wobbles off to seek the solace offered by the nearest human male. "The cat swore at me," the dog will tattle. At which time the human male will sympathize, scratch the dog behind the ears, and observe something like, "That naughty kitty."

The cat, for whom expletives are mother's milk, will then call the dog something which in cat language translates as "large orifice," lick its paws once or twice as a reminder, turn, and walk calmly off, its tail flourishing in the feline equivalent of "giving the finger."

Swearing is unheard of on Pluto, and as a result dogs have no recourse to it. After all, what would a dog call something or someone it hated? It wouldn't do to call something a female dog or a son of a female dog when in fact the dog itself is either one or the other. And "female cat" does not have the same ring, somehow.

Sexual epithets, plentiful in Saturnian, are similarly missing weapons in a dog's arsenal. For a dog, sex of whatever kind is simply a pleasurable act, and wishing intercourse upon another would be taken more as a gracious pleasantry than a threat. Nor will a dog utter a blasphemy; dogs are true believers and do not utter the name of the Almighty except in reverence. When a dog barks or otherwise communicates to human beings verbally, it is speaking plain Plutonian: "Watch out, the garbage guy is stealing our garbage again." Or, "The mail person is attacking. I'm warning you."

Dogs can be hurt by profanities, however, coming either from a cat or from a human being. Being called a son of a female dog by a man seems shameful, even if it is literally true. Moreover, profanity is entirely unnecessary in chastising a dog for bad behavior. Merely speaking in a loud voice is enough to make the dog feel guilty, even if it's not.

Cats, on the other hand, know no guilt. They carry out nasty acts with aplomb and swear like longshoremen. Anyone who has heard a couple cats outside late at night, screeching and yowling, should be forewarned: it doesn't matter whether they are fighting or making love. Their language is equally deplorable in either case. Cover your children's ears.

COMMUNICATING WITH HUMAN BEINGS

> The capacity of human beings to bore one another seems to be vastly greater than that of any other animal.
> — *H. L. Mencken*

Cats carried with them from Saturn the ability to read minds. As a result, they pay little attention to what a human being actually says. They know that "Here, Kitty, Kitty," can mean anything from "I have a lovely bowl of cream for you," to "You miserable, filthy beast, when I catch you I'm going to throw you in the bathtub and scrub you until you molt." It is not the words, but the intent behind the words, that they hear.

Furthermore, they ignore imperative constructions entirely. "If it doesn't have a subject, blow it off," is their rude response. Such clauses as "Come here," "Get off the table," or "Get out of my chair," consequently, are of no effect whatever. They do understand violence, however, and will respond to commands if punctuated by a swift kick.

Unlike dogs, their response to violence is not guilt, but resentment. They will retaliate if pushed. If you come to breakfast some morning to find your linen napkin shredded, think back: Did you encourage the animal rather vigorously to get its hinder off your dinner plate last night? Vengeance is mine, saith the cat.

Those experienced in working with cats will counsel patience, meaning "Let the cat walk over you, because if you don't, it will walk over you anyway." It will, for example, climb into your lap and demand that you pet it, even if you would rather read your book. It simply will not accept, and cannot even imagine, that any book can be as fascinating as a cat in your lap.

If you give in and set your book aside to administer a full massage, you will be rewarded

**An exercise in Plutonian grammar:
"(Who/Whom) is taking (who/whom) for a walk?**

with a purr. Do not be misled into thinking that this Mack Truck motor sound translates into gratitude. In Saturnian it means something closer to "Sucker-r-r-r-r-r-r-r-r-r-r-r-r-r-r-r." Contentment is being registered, albeit with the ever-present feline disdain. Not for a cat the cud-chewing contentment of a cow; a cat can not feel real satisfaction unless it knows it has come at someone else's expense.

In the lap-sit position, cats are given to kneading your thighs. Unless you are wearing heavy canvas underwear, this action can prove painful. Try to remember that this habit is instinctual and should not be taken personally. Cats are simply expressing affection by sinking their claws into your flesh.

Whatever you do, avoid cringing, jerking in anguish, or otherwise disturbing Kitty while she is undertaking Saturnian acupuncture. She may take such movements as a rebuke of her talents as a seamstress and leap suddenly from your lap in the feline equivalent of "laying rubber."

If your thighs are not made of asphalt and you are reluctant to have them used as a launching pad, remain completely still while undergoing body piercing and try to think of the alternative. Cats are renowned for their drag-racing ability (see "Off The Wall," below), and will "scratch gravel" in vital regions without so much as a thank you.

In contrast to cats, dogs are slavish in their gratitude, even for the tiniest morsel of attention. Toss them a crumb, you are a friend for life; they will wag their tails off. More lavish care earns ever more exaggerated devotion. On the inflated Plutonian scale, anyone who pays attention earns at least a B-plus. Anyone who goes beyond mere tolerance gets an A. From there on, the grade is simply decorated with additional pluses. The dog's master earns A-plus-plus-plus-plus-plus, *ad infinitum* or until they both lose track of the count.

A cat, of course, doesn't have a master, or a mistress either, for that matter, and uses a rather flat grade scale ranging from a high of C to a low of D-minus. Forget F; any lower than D-minus, and the cat is out of here like a rocket.

Grammar is important in speaking to a dog. Do not tell your dog to "set" or "lay." Its response is likely to be a stare, which like all Plutonian stares, carries great significance. What the dog is attempting to tell you is this: "I'm terribly sorry, but I am neither the sun nor a hen. If you wish me to perform, try using 'sit' or 'lie.'"

Of course, a dog may not obey you even when you use correct grammar, but it will admire your intelligence. A cat, on the contrary, feels grammar is beneath it, and will neither obey you nor respect you for applying it.

A dog enjoys the finer points of grammar, as well, such as the proper use of "who" and "whom," as in the sentence, "Who is taking whom for a walk?" "Who" is on one end of the

The Meaningful Stare

leash, and "whom" is on the other end; the question is which has the greater will power.

Here is a grammatical problem that can keep a dog entranced for hours: "Rex is one of those dogs that (is/are) always barking." Some say that, since Rex is just one dog, the proper verb form should be "is." Others contend that, since the antecedent for "that" is the plural "dogs," the proper verb form should be "are." Still others insist that, if Rex keeps on barking, he will be one of those dogs that (is/are) dead.

Humans are often surprised to learn of a dog's concern for grammar, considering its lack of scruples in other areas. One theory is that dogs were held back twice in fifth grade on Pluto and consequently got a triple dose of basic grammar from that kindly-but-stern prune-faced teacher everybody has in fifth grade. They were so drilled that grammar became second nature, like scratching ears.

Cats, many of whom have been to college, are cavalier about grammar. They are among those creatures who believe using "ain't" is cute, and they would rather eat dry food than hear the phrase "his or her," as it is applied merely to be grammatically as well as politically correct. They are, therefore, capable of sentences such as this one: "Every cat prefers their own bed." Even journalistic cats commit such sentences without blinking. And they have nothing but scorn for any dog who tries to correct them.

Body language is important to dogs, as well. You often will catch your dog reading your posture and your gestures, especially if the time is near for a walk or a feeding. Your efforts to loosen tight underclothing or to whisk away a bothersome insect will often be interpreted by your dog as relevant to the dog's well-being. "Are we going, then?" it seems to be saying. "Is it time? You want me to fetch the leash?"

At such times, you must preserve the ambiguous serenity of a Buddha, make no sudden movements, and assume a fixed, benign smile. All this your dog will interpret as meaning that either your brain has gone soft or your watch is broken, and it will return to its tense vigil.

The Meaningful Stare is a staple of dog communication, and is especially apparent when it is watching someone eat meat. Roughly translated, it means "I am devoted to you and ask so very little in return. Do what you want, but do try to remember your low-cholesterol diet. Please continue to stuff your face; I'll just watch. No, really, just ignore my protruding ribs. And that time I pushed you out of the path of an oncoming truck, don't give it another thought."

This silent monolog will continue until you give the dog a small corner of your ham sandwich, at which point the dog will snarf down the morsel in a fraction of a second and begin all over again: "I am devoted to you and ask so very little in return . . ."

The Saturnian equivalent of the Meaningful Stare is the Halloween Stance: back arched, hair erect, puffed up all over, gentle Tabby masquerading as mountain lion. The cat version of

Halloween Cat

"trick-or-treat" is roughly interpreted as "Give me a treat or I'll kill you." The stance is used widely to intimidate dogs, who get spooked by anything that can assume the shape of a horseshoe without doing damage to the spinal column.

SELF-ESTEEM

> To his dog, every man is Napoleon;
> hence the constant popularity of dogs.
> — *Aldous Huxley*

This one, as No-Brainers say, is a no-brainer. Cats have it, dogs don't. Cats are up to any honor, and about time; dogs are unworthy. The medal or statue has not been created that sufficiently acknowledges the honor that a cat believes it is due; for a dog, every little pat is the Academy Award and the Congressional Medal of Honor.

In its acceptance speech, a cat may thank "the little people" who helped to get it where it is today, but with obvious insincerity; a dog will go on and on, naming anybody remotely associated with it, its mother, its father, its brothers and sisters, its master, its mistress, the wonderful vet, the talented cast, the technical creators, the set designer, the agent, the rest of the pups in obedience school, its trainer, its friends, especially . . . until it is dragged off the stage, still trying to wedge in one more name.

THE GREAT DEBATE

POLITICS

> America is a large, friendly dog in a very small room. Every time it wags its tail, it knocks over a chair.
> — *Arnold Joseph Toynbee*

> If you want a friend in Washington, buy a dog.
> — *attributed to Harry Truman by Bill Clinton, although the attribution has been disputed by cats in Congress*

Cats, especially fat ones, are inclined to be Republicans, although by nature they are not joiners. They believe in free trade and the open marketplace as long as they profit by it. They want to keep government out of their fur and favor a tax system which appears to split the tax burden equally while really being so complicated that clever cat attorneys can find loopholes which will prevent cats from paying anything at all. They would prefer a sales tax (or dog tax, as they refer to it among themselves) rather than an income tax, since cats spend very little.

They are social conservatives and are against birth control, the theory of evolution, global warming, affirmative action, government-subsidized art, and anything for which there seems to be a logical argument or substantial scientific support.

Actually, the first immigrants from Saturn were royalists and many of their offspring remain Tories today, although somewhat frustrated by the irrefutable logic that says they can't all be royalty. They solve the problem by subdividing the territory into domains called "households" in which a cat may serve as king or queen. If there are more cats than one in a household, one seizes the crown by *coup d'etat* and makes the others his subjects, although they all get to be aristocrats, dukes, duchesses, counts, countesses, earls and earlesses.

If they run out of titles, they make them up, like "The Second Brouhaha of Sycamore" or "The Grand Galluph of Elm." The roles of serfs, peasants, and commoners may be taken only by human beings and dogs.

That suits dogs just fine, since they are all in fact from good peasant stock to begin with and are now, for the most part, staunch Democrats of the old school. They believe in organizing to demand justice, which they see tipping rather heavily in favor of the rich and powerful cats. They support a steeply graduated income tax which sticks it to the fat cats and which provides special exemptions for large litters of puppies, veterans of the hunt, and runts.

They favor social programs providing a safety net for strays and single dams with small pups (ADDP), and veterinary benefits for the elderly. They seek legislation which controls unwarranted use of concealed weapons, and would secretly like to see all cats declawed.

Dogs have trouble, however, keeping their ranks joined, and are often splintered by single-issue voting (anti-birth-control as a notable example) and by confusion among working dogs who think that they must do anything to protect their jobs, even if it means selling out to the fat cats. Many have bought into the old slogan, "What's good for Tabby is good for Fido, too," or as it is known in political circles, the "piddle-down" principle. As a result, dogs have lost the political clout they once had and face years of rebuilding the old coalition with gerbils, hamsters, green turtles, and other lesser household pets.

As this is written, cats control congress, dogs the administration. During the first term of President Clinton, the sad truth for dogs was that there was a cat in the White House, serving as a major presidential advisor and flaunting a long tradition of Democratic dogs like Roosevelt's Fala and Johnson's beagles. (Okay, there was Checkers, but he was brought in to demonstrate that Nixon was moral, uprighteous, and honest; everybody knows he was a ringer.)

During his second term, Clinton got himself a dog, apparently in an attempt to redefine himself as moral, uprighteous, and honest. This event threw congressional cats into an uproar, with many demanding that the attorney general appoint a special counsel to look into charges (made by congressional cats) that Clinton intended to let the dog sleep in the Lincoln bedroom and bury its bones at Arlington. Sources close to the investigation said Socks had been wired to record the president talking baby-talk to a pup. Radio talk show host Rush Limpup went further yet, suggesting that the dog was female and might end up in Clinton's own bed.

A poodle made a public statement that Clinton had attempted to force his attentions on her when he was still governor (which she of course rebuffed, since she was apolitical). At a congressional hearing, a pekinese admitted that he had contributed several thousand dollars to the

Trading insults with a squirrel.

Clinton campaign in return for presidential doggy treats, namely, a corner on the market in pigs' ears.

Even rank-and-file union dogs, remembering Checkers, had to wonder. After all, the previous president, a Republican, hated broccoli, just as dogs do, and favored dogs, one of whom, Millie, authored a major book that cast him in a flattering light. And they frankly do not know what to make of a potential candidate, the current vice president, who looks like a tree and has the demeanor of a fire plug. It was all as though suddenly the law of gravity had been repealed and up was down and dogs could fly and cats could do an honest day's work.

What is a dog to think, anymore? Perhaps it is time after all for a third party, led, let us say, by a sharp-tongued Chihuahua who could win votes both from self-interested cats (the only kind, really) and disaffected dogs with the canny use of charts and graphs. Dogs would be fascinated by the bright colors and cats would watch the pointer carefully, assuming someone was attempting to play with them.

RECREATION

Exercise is important for both Saturnians and Plutonians, but for different reasons. For one thing, neither race thinks of exercise the way humans do, as "vigorous activity necessary for the well-being of

Off the Wall

the physique which we will undertake against our wills because if we don't we will die before we can start collecting on that 401K we've been contributing to all these years."

Dogs enjoy exercise for its own sake, and indeed they do not think of it as exercise at all. They think of it as "getting outside to see what's been going on and at the same time harassing any smaller creatures that may pop up." In short, exercise for a dog is actually fun. The thoughtful dog owner will contribute to the fun by entering more fully into the spirit of the occasion and refrain from grousing when the animal decorates a neighbor's yard with doo-doo or when it stops by every tree and hydrant to smell the news of the day and to examine the personal columns in the want ads.

Dogs prefer not to be on a leash, but they are by nature respectful of the law and will abide by local ordinances willingly if their masters cut them a little slack. They prefer a "gentleman's agreement" which acknowledges that man and dog have vastly different ideas about what constitutes a "walk." If necessary, they will accede to a written contract which reads something like this:

> AGREEMENT between Rex, hereinafter to be known as THE DOG and Joe Blau, hereinafter to be known as THE MAN, regarding the activity undertaken two (2) times per day hereinafter to be known as THE WALK:
> THE DOG swears and attests and all that other legal stuff
> 1. that THE DOG will submit to the leash and collar if allowed at least eight (8) times during THE WALK to stop and peruse a sapling or a random clump of grass for a period of no less that three (3) minutes each for signs of life that may be related or in some other way of interest to THE DOG.
> 2. that THE DOG will spend at least forty (40) percent of THE WALK adhering to sidewalks, marked trails, and other accepted routes of human conveyance, with the rest of THE WALK dedicated to the really exciting activities of sniffing, peeing, digging, and

Hatching an Awk.

chasing after every animal of a size commensurate with THE DOG's confidence in its ability to make the animal run.

3. that THE DOG will refrain from eating any tasty cat poop that it may come upon in its explorations if THE MAN can assure it that immediately upon completion of THE WALK it will be fed treats such as biscuits, hog's ears, or actual meat or meat byproducts that have taste and nutritional equivalent to aforesaid cat poop.

4. that THE DOG will refrain from rolling on the remains of anonymous dead animals for the purpose of attaining a charnel house

aura particularly pleasing to its kind provided that THE MAN will stop gagging and will put off its bath for a few more days.

5. that THE DOG will not make a fool of itself with any Plutonian of the opposite gender it many encounter on THE WALK, on the condition that THE MAN promises to participate in some activity of equivalent pleasure for THE DOG, most particularly the game of fetch, which game to be constituted of at least fifty (50) separate and distinct throws of a stick, a ball, or a Frisbee.

6. that THE DOG will spend no more than five (5) minutes barking at the obnoxious chattering squirrel so long as THE MAN limits his boring discussions with other humans he encounters on THE WALK to the same duration.

Such contracts make life easier for both dogs and humans by setting precisely how far each will put up with the nonsense of the other. Of course, the dog would much prefer to roam on his own without such curbs on his activities, and luxuries such as large fenced back yards, visits to the farm, and hunting and fishing trips allow the fullest expression of Plutonian recreation.

Given the freedom, dogs would devote all their time to exploring the great Mysteries of Life, chief among which is how squirrels vanish while being chased around a tree and then miraculously reappear a few moments later in the branches of that tree. The puzzlement is aggravated by the squirrel's tendency to jeer and cast aspersions on the intelligence of dogs, all the time flourishing its ridiculous tail like a battle flag. Some dogs try to maintain their composure under such circumstances, but most give in to the temptation to exchange insults, even though they know they will come out on the short end.

> SQUIRREL: Hey, dog, why don't you go back to the brain factory and ask for an extension on your warranty?
> DOG: Oh yeah? Well, why don't you go back to the tail factory and ask for an extension on your dumb tail?
> SQUIRREL: Is that your idea of a retort, dog, or are you just jealous? What happened to your tail, anyway? Did you back into an electric fan?
> DOG: Did you back into a toaster?
> SQUIRREL: Why don't you back into a broom handle. You could be a dog on a stick.
> DOG: Oh Yeah?

A cat views recreation in a much different light. The game of fetch is out of the question, since it would amount to an admission of subservience. When a ball is thrown, a cat will pursue it, but then it will settle on it as though attempting to hatch it. This peculiar behavior has been explained by Saturnian experts as a reflection of cat survival on that distant planet. The Awk, an ungainly, flightless species somewhat resembling a bird, often would lay its eggs on the slopes of mountains. During the frequent windstorms that beset Saturn, primitive cats would often wait for the nests to be jiggled loose, at which times the eggs would spill out and

**Cat on a leash:
an activity much resembling kite flying**

roll down the mountain, the cats in pursuit, as fast as they could drag their tails. If a cat caught up with an Awk egg, it would not waste time attempting to crack it open, since the shell is extremely thick and tough. Instead, the cat would sit on the egg until it was hatched, at which time it would eat the newborn Awk with relish and a little mustard.

The Awk did not make the trip to earth, although its reputation as a clumsy, unfortunate beast was known of and discussed among the intelligentsia. It survives today chiefly as a notation by college professors in the margins of student themes, along with *Nota Bene*, an inhabitant of Jupiter. Sometimes the notation appears by itself, sometimes as "Damn Awk," a reminder that the beast deserved extinction.

The Saturnian equivalent of "fetch" is "Off the Wall," which has the advantage, from the cat's point of view, of not requiring human participation. Just as cats know when to stop eating, as dogs do not, so cats know when they need some physical exercise. At such times they engage in "Off the Wall," which somewhat resembles the human games of handball or paddleball, with the cat taking the role of the ball. Acceleration counts for much in this game, and zero-to-fifty in two seconds is regarded as minimum. As the cat caroms off walls, doors, and furniture, it sometimes seems to exceed the speed of light and to disappear completely in a warp-three blur. Such games seldom last more than five minutes, however, since the whole point of the game is to finish quickly so the cat can get back to more serious endeavors such as sleeping.

Cats once spent much time outdoors and in rural communities were left to roam free so that they could catch mice. Mousing did not come naturally to a cat, of course, and was rather frustrating for mice and cats both because once caught, mice refused to hatch, and when eaten had a horrible mousy taste not at all resembling tuna. The cat often would leave the wounded and bleeding mouse by the kitchen step and then go off in search of birds.

Birds are to cats what squirrels are to dogs. Cats can't stand the fact that birds can fly longer than they can and that birds do not have to be rescued from high trees by the fire department. This natural enmity, combined with racial memories of the Awk, made for an untenable situation. Bird lovers lobbied for decades to have cats contained inside houses and apartments, and in our age have largely achieved this goal. Recreation for cats, therefore, has become an even greater challenge for cat owners.

Some people, feeling that they are somehow depriving the cat of a total experience, try putting a collar and a leash on a cat and take it for a stroll outside, as they would a dog. This is a mistake. Taking a cat for a walk on a leash is an activity akin to flying a kite. The cat tends to become airborne when restrained in any way. If the intention is merely to provide physical exercise for the cat, the purpose is served, but at a terrible cost to human dignity. The cat will crash for two days afterwards, and the experience is not one likely to be repeated. The cat leash is put to much better use as a dance partner for the cat.

Yes, cats love to dance, as many people discover almost by accident when trailing a piece of string around after opening a package. String, which by Saturnian definition is any long flexible object capable of being scooted along the floor or whipped through the air, can provide hours of dancing pleasure to any cat.

The object of a cat's pursuit of string may seem at first simply to catch it, but a little experimentation proves that to be far from the case. A piece of string caught is an inert thing, without interest. It becomes apparent in a short while that the dance of pursuit rather than capture is the end being sought. It is "art for art's sake." Masters of the dance are advised, therefore, to use a material that is resistant to the grasp of cat claws. The author advises the use of that plastic strapping tape that binds mail-order goods. This tape retains the sinuous quality held dear by cats while remaining almost perfectly elusive.

Proper string handling is important, as well. Simply dragging the string about is deadly dull.

Trailing it along in a short arc and finishing with an upward motion produces the best flourishes. The cat ballerina will soon be performing pirouettes and spectacular leaps that would do justice to Russian companies. Strictly speaking, perhaps, the result is closer to Modern Dance than to classical ballet, since it derives more from the subjective impulses of the performer. Nevertheless, the sight of a cat engaged in terpsichore to the accompaniment of classical music is inspiring and almost makes up for the total physical collapse wrought upon the human being involved.

PHILOSOPHY

> The privilege of absurdity; to which no living creature is subject but man only.
> —*Thomas Hobbes*

Cats, when they give philosophy any thought at all, find that they lean naturally toward the DesCartesian dictum, "I eat, therefore I am." This proposition has the feline advantage of containing the word "I" in it twice, along with the word "eat," both expressions favored by Saturnians everywhere. Some have suggested changing the word "am" to "sleep," so that the motto would contain three good cat words instead of two, but that suggestion has failed to win the attention of cats who were sleeping or very drowsy when the idea was first mentioned.

Societally, cats support a *laissez faire* policy, by which they mean "Leave ME alone," or "Don't call me, I'll call you." They tend to embrace metaphysics rather than epistemology or aesthetics. For a cat the philosophical conundrum "How do you know you know?" has little meaning. "I know because I am a cat, Dummy." And art is any representation in which cats are the principle subjects. They know what they like, and "Poker-Playing Pups" is too *gauche* for their tastes. They cite it as the most obvious and ridiculous example when the National Endowment for Doggy Art is seeking public funding.

Metaphysics, the philosophical branch devoted to the search of the basic worldstuff, is something cats can really sink their teeth into, however, because they believe that the indivisible substance of the world is not an atomic particle, but tuna in oil. The argument supporting this premise is rather hard to follow, but the gist is that cats love tuna and can't imagine a universe without it; therefore, the universe is tuna. It follows that when cats die, they go neither to to heaven or hell, neither do they return to dust; they return to tuna. This belief accounts for the relative fearlessness of cats, even when they've expended eight of their nine lives.

Dogs are Platonists, mostly because Plato reminds them of Pluto. Nevertheless, they genuinely believe in idealism, as far as they can understand it. The way they get it, everything that exists in this world has its perfected counterpart or ideal in a world beyond. That would mean that somewhere there exists a perfect dried hog's ear. Enough said.

They are attracted, as well to the notion that truth, beauty, and goodness are one in the same. It's easy to remember and agrees with the Plutonian perception: for example, a dried hog's ear is good, therefore it is also true and beautiful.

As for metaphysics, dogs adhere to Epicurus' concept of atoms as the building blocks of the universe. It's the plutonium talking, of course.

EMBARRASSING BEHAVIOR

> Man is the only animal that blushes. Or
> needs to.
> — *Mark Twain*

The first question to ask with regard to this topic is "From whose point of view?" What is embarrassing to a human being may be simply satisfying to a dog or cat.

A cat finds people embarrassing, annoyingly so, if they speak baby-talk to a dog. A dog, on the other hand, finds only other dogs embarrassing, especially when they put on airs and pretend to be better than they are. For a golden retriever, a poodle is embarrassing *per se*.

Basset embarrassed by its own ears.

A basset finds its own ears embarrassing; you can see it in its eyes.

All parties are embarrassed, of course, when human beings force dogs to wear clothing of any kind. A boxer dressed in a vest and tie is an em-

Plutonian greeting plays badly on Earth.

barrassment to nature itself, as is any dog wearing knitted booties.

We will restrict ourselves in this section, therefore, to the behavior of dogs and cats that brings embarrassment to the human beings with whom the animals are closely associated. Most behavior of this kind has sexual overtones. Let us begin with the dog who greets a guest at the door by thrusting its nose into the guest's crotch.

Even veterinarians and animal psychologists have no decent explanation for this act, although many suspect that it is an old Plutonian custom that has translated rather badly to our planet. Everyone has seen two dogs sidle up to each other and sniff each other's hindquarters. That is simply the Plutonian way of saying, "How ARE you?!"

The difficulty arises when the creature being greeted stands erect on two feet, thus allowing the dog more direct access to the source of its curiosity. You could ask your guest to drop to his knees and sniff back, which of course would be the proper Plutonian response, but which could lead to further complications. There remains, then, only a handful of solutions, from which you may choose one that seems to you most appropriate:

☛ **Try to ignore it**. This course is easier, unfortunately, for the person whose dog it is than for the guest with the wet muzzle embedded in his or her groin.

☞ **Launch a preemptive strike.** If you are in the position of the attackee, you might lift your knee quickly and allow it to connect smartly with the dog's chin, at the same time giggling as though preternaturally ticklish. This action, which has the advantage of seeming believable, almost reflexive, has the additional merit of being conclusive, since the dog will probably retire to mediate upon the question, "What hit me?"

☞ **Make light of it.** This solution is, once again, easier for the dog owner, who might memorize a number of *bon mots* with which to regale his guest. Here is a brief sampling: "Ha ha. Sorry, Rex is trained to sniff out drugs. You must have some pot on you." Or, "Ha ha, Rex wants a treat. Do you have a jellybean in your pocket?" Or, "Ha ha. Rex is a pointer. He always gets his bird." Under no circumstances must the introductory "Ha ha" be omitted, since it alerts the guest to the fact that you are being amusing rather than stupid. If there remains some doubt, add a "Ha ha" onto the end, as well.

☞ **Apologize and/or lie.** Since a simple apology will rarely do, it usually must be accompanied by prevarication. The good news here is that almost any lie will do. It doesn't have to be believable, since embarrassed humans are willing to accept any explanation, no matter how far-fetched, rather than the obvious one.

Try one of these: "I'm terribly sorry, but Rex has lost the sight in one eye and has trouble judging distances. He keeps running into things." Or, "You have to forgive Rex, he hasn't been the same since the operation. He had his appendix removed and keeps looking for it everywhere." Or, "Poor Rex. He froze his nose last winter sniffing a hydrant and has been desperate to get it warm ever since."

All of these lies incorporate an element of sympathy for the dog as a preventative of major violence directed toward the animal. Beware, however, if the attackee inquires, "Which eye is the good one," or "Which side is the appendix on, again?" and then takes a few swings with his foot as though practicing a drop kick.

Once in a while the guest will be someone you would like to get rid of — an IRS agent, for example, or a distributor of religious tracts. In that case, your dog's bad habit might become a boon.

The effect can be enhanced by subtly suggesting that your dog's friendly welcome is actually aggressive and threatening: "Back Fang! Don't go for body parts until I signal!" Or you might inquire of the interloper, "Have you been protected against rabies? Fang hasn't been the same

Pedro practicing to be a bicycle clip.

since he had that scrap with a skunk." Or, "Whatever you do, don't let him know you fear him! He smelled sweat on a Jehovah's Witness last month and put a severe dent in our liability insurance."

Cats have their little behavioral quirks, as well, needless to say. Not the least of these is their tendency to flounce around like waterfront trollops. "Hey sailor, want to party? Take a look at what's under the tail, big guy. You got a motel room or what?"

This mode overtakes cats at the most inopportune times, such as when you are entertaining clergy. It is impossible to prevent a kindly man or woman of the cloth from attempting to pet the creature, even though you know that the cat's response will be to arch upward under the ordained palm in a paroxysm of delight, as though to say, "Whoa, you got a nice touch on you, Ducky. Rub me there again, I'm yours."

Your options are severely limited under these conditions. No use pretending something is not going on or that it means something else, and apologies would serve only to call further attention to it and invite conversation on the subject.

The following solution, while untested, seems your only alternative: Murmur something ambiguous like, "My, Monsignor, you have quite a way with animals. Excuse me, Buffy is late for her tennis lessons." Then scoop up the cat and take it into the bedroom where it can be locked in the closet or, better yet, strangled.

Don't worry about charges of cat abuse or committing a mortal sin. There is no court in the land — not one familiar with the curious ways of cats, a least — that would convict you. And the bishop would surely be willing to secure for you a papal pardon.

While most other perceived transgressions of cats pale by comparison to the one discussed above, regurgitating loudly during the weekly bridge game offers a challenge to even the most creative Saturnian apologist.

Once again, direct action, rather than bunco or ineffective mendacity, is the order of the day. Round up the offending, *i.e.*, gagging, animal, transport it a safe distance from the house, stuff it with *plastique*, and explode it. And remember, all this might have been prevented if in the first place you had listened to your heart and had secreted the cat in a trunk in the attic until the bridge game blew over.

There remains then, the *sine qua non* of disgusting habits by animals: leg humping. Even the most experienced of pet handlers have thrown in the towel on this one. There is nothing, I repeat, *nothing* you can do or say that will in any way get you out of this corner. Will you die of embarrassment? Very well, then, say your prayers and breathe your last.

Or do you really think a guest will buy the ruse that your fox terrier has been in training to be a bicycle clip? Or that its weight-reduction program calls for vigorous push-ups? I didn't think so.

Very well, then, accept it. Acknowledge it. "The filthy beast seems to want to have intercourse with your shin. Would you like me to have it destroyed?"

This frank approach saves you the trouble of telling lies and making them jibe with the truth, and seldom will a guest demand the death sentence. If such a demand is made, and you haven't the stomach for it, buy the pooch a steamship ticket to Buenos Aires. He will find the food there to his liking, and the other Plutonians who have been similarly deported will join him daily at the expatriate club for cocktails, chicken wings, and good conversation.

CAREERS FOR CATS

Professional men, they have no cares;
whatever happens, they get theirs.
— *Ogden Nash*

Dogs have jobs; cats have careers. Dogs make good hunters, good foot soldiers, good cops. Cats prefer the professions: medicine (although their prescriptions usually have to do with licking something), politics, and especially law.

The shyster gene is deeply embedded in the Saturnian DNA. At night one hears them —

when not engaged in making feline woo or fighting — pleading their cases. They excel in the defense of their fellowcats and in the prosecution of dogs. The result is that ordinary prisons are overcrowded with dogs, while cats are to be found incarcerated only in the country club institutions in which white-collar criminals serve out their mild reprimands.

There are no cats on death row; their cat lawyers got them off, alleging temporary insanity (easy enough to believe about cats), insufficient evidence (the defendant having eaten it), or lack of motive (the defendant even now exhibiting the unmistakable signs of not being moved to do much of anything).

Cat lawyers, faced with the undeniable guilt of their clients, sometimes have to resort to bribing jurors (who, being mostly cats, are easily bought), "playing the race card" (*i.e.*, alleging centuries of bigotry which presumed cats to be satanic, familiars of witches and warlocks, much given to black magic), or, in really desperate straits, casting a spell upon the court.

Cat lawyers often graduate to the role of judge, for which they are perfectly suited, especially in their drowsy-eyed meditative mode immediately preceding or immediately following a nap. Being a judge leaves a cat with nothing much to do, which suits the cat just fine. It can doze off during testimony, be aroused during

Cats make good judges.

closing arguments, and come wide awake and testy during sentencing, the better to savor hitting the miscreant Fido with life imprisonment or reducing poor Tabby's incarceration to time served.

Some Saturnian lawyers run for public office, although they are distrustful of the democratic process and will accept nomination only in districts properly gerrymandered so that dogs are in the distinct minority.

Once in office, cats will devote themselves to campaign fund-raising, securing favorable legislation for their most prosperous donors, and voting the party line (see above under Politics).

When they retire, if they have managed to avoid impeachment, they will donate their papers (minus the self-incriminating reams, of course) to a library named for them. At that point they take on the mantle of "elder statescat," which means that they dispense bad advice to their successors without fear of retaliation.

CATS AND DOGS IN LANGUAGE: A SELECTIVE GLOSSARY

> Spoken language is merely a series of squeaks.
> — *Alfred North Whitehead*

A boy and his dog — An annoyance and its aggravation.

Catatonic — Insensible and inert, like a cat who has just had a heavy meal.

Catalog — A list of virtues; for and of cats, a very long list.

Catalyst — A cat who precipitates a divorce in order to be the sole object of its mistress's adoration.

Concatenation

Catechism — Questions and answers about cats: Are cats wise? Yes. Do cats like tuna? Yes. Are dogs evil? Emphatically yes. Used to indoctrinate kittens.

CAT-scan — A sleepy-eyed stare given by a cat toward a dog or human it does not trust.

Catgut — Evidence that cats once played tennis or the violin or engaged in angling; replaced in this age by nylon or other synthetic feline intestinal material without any corresponding improvement in sports or music.

Category — Class; cats have it, dogs do not.

Cater — Serve the needs of a cat; tuna on rye will do just dandy, thank you. Hold the rye.

Caterwaul — 1. An aria sung by a Saturnian diva pleading for union with the heavyset baritone, or with any baritone, or tenor, or bass. 2. The sound of catclaws raking slate.

Cat's cradle — 1. A game played with string, a material much beloved among cats for its ability to entertain. 2. A lap.

Cat's paw — A dupe, a dope, a creature easily used; i.e., a dog.

Concatenation — A cat fight.

Catastrophe — A calamity; what a cat senses when he hears the human utterance "We're out of tuna."

Catbird — A bird that sounds like a cat; not to be confused with the cat at the window, watching the bird feeder and emitting a horrible, birdlike chirp, with the apparent intention of attracting sparrows to its vicinity.

Cat Dream — indicated by absolute immobility. Cats have three kinds of dreams: 1. Good Dream — dreaming it is eating; 2. Better Dream — dreaming it is sitting on a lap; 3. Best Dream — dreaming it is sleeping.

Cat nap — A brief sleep; for a cat, any doze under five hours duration.

Curtail — To lop off; taken from the old practice of removing a cur's tail and burying it under the front porch to prevent it from running away; for some reason, dogs objected to this practice and suggested that they would gladly stay home if the cat's tail were removed instead.

Dog Days — The hot days of summer, so-called because they offer everyone an opportunity to feel like a dog. They also have something to do with the Dog Star, Lassie.

Dog dream — Indicated by RLM (Rapid Leg Movement). Dogs have two kinds of dreams: 1. Good Dream — dreaming it is chasing a rabbit; 2. Bad Dream — dreaming it is being chased by a rabbit.

Dognap — To steal a dog for purposes of securing a ransom; an unprofitable criminal enterprise.

Dog collar — A device worn by Plutonian clerics.

Good Dog Dream

Doggerel —

> A kind of rhyme
> that we know well,
> Goes by the name
> of doggerel.

> Dogs make verse
> and cats do, too,
> but dogs do worse
> as doggies do.

Actually, cats write only free verse.

Dogmatic — Given to slavish adherence to rules made up by others; a religious dog.

Bad Dog Dream

Dogged — Stubborn dedication to a cause, like a dog searching for just the right place to lie down.

Doggy bag — A bag containing food which will never reach the mouth of a dog; it will be consumed immediately by the human being who had feigned satiety or left behind in the car, where it will be discovered when it rots.

Dog's age — A long time, longer than a coon's age, shorter than a man's age. The length of time it takes for a dog to get smart.

Fetch — An excellent recreation for dogs, provided they can train their masters to throw a stick repeatedly.

Plutonian Howdy

Fleas — The only common threat to cats and dogs. Fleas are to cats and dogs what the atomic bomb is to humankind: the great hope for world peace.

Hair of the dog — A sip of the poison that killed you last night. Caution: Many start with the hair and end with the whole dog.

Hang-dog look — Expression assumed by a dog after having been caught attempting to microwave the cat.

Lap dog — A perversion; a dog that behaves like a cat.

Moon dog — A dog that sticks its tail out the car window instead of its head. This behavior is referred to by teenaged dogs as "making a statement."

New trick — Behavior that cannot be taught to an old dog, or to a cat of any age.

Nine lives — An old wives' tradition that grew out of the fact that cats lie about their age. The average cat past puberty will shave off at least five years. Dogs, on the other hand, will actually add to their age under the mistaken belief that age brings respect and wisdom. The startling result of these opposed practices is that there are no middle-aged cats and dogs.

Saturnian Curl

Plutocracy — The oppressive rule of a dog who has attained wealth. While dogs are rarely wealthy, those who have made out in the stock market belong always among the boorish *nouveau riche* who insist upon using money to cow (or to avoid sexism, bully) those less wealthy. *Cf.* cats, who maintain an oppressive rule even though broke. Cats are aristocrats and like many human aristocrats, temporarily without funds, but poverty does not reduce the ego of a cat. Among dogs, the poodle, the pekinese, the doberman pinscher, and the afghan hound are breeds particularly given to plutocracy.

Plutonian howdy — The traditional plutonian greeting: two dogs stretched end to end.

Poodle Cut — A fashion perpetrated upon unwitting animals by effete French hairdressers who have dogs confused with decorative shrubs.

Putting on the dog — 1. Dressing up, like a dog in a tuxedo. 2. Conning the canine, a pastime for cats.

Saturnian curl — The standard position for cat naps; one cat laid end to end.

Saturnine — Leaden, cold, and gloomy, like a cat contemplating dry food containing no tuna.

Muttnik — A dog in orbit. In the early stages of the exploration of space it was considered appropriate to send a dog "where no dog had gone before," just in case there was something out there that might not agree with John Glenn. It should be noted that the dog did not do this willingly, since dogs are afraid of flying and believe that experiments involving centrifugal force should be limited to spinning cats around by the tail, as has often been undertaken by young males of the human persuasion.

Tomcat — 1. Noun; a male cat that has not been to the vet to become a naturalized citizen. 2. Verb; to pursue the female of the species with an enthusiasm reminiscent of certain Democratic presidents. In fact, a national campaign is under way to replace the term with the more redolent one "Kennedycat."

Wag — 1. Verb; a dog's expression of joy over anything more pleasurable than a swift kick. 2. Noun; a dog moved to laughter by his own tale.

CATS AND DOGS IN LITERATURE

> As for the dog, he jumped out of the ship himself, and swam on shore to me the day after I went on shore with my first cargo, and was a trusty servant to me many years. I wanted nothing that he could fetch me, nor any company that he could make up to me; I only wanted to have him talk to me, but that would not do.
> —Daniel Defoe, *Robinson Crusoe*

Odysseus' old dog Argus set a high literary standard by looking up from where he was reclining on a dung heap, spotting his master after a 20-year absence, giving his tail a feeble wag, and dying. This noble gesture of endurance and loyalty has been cited for centuries in dogdom as an epitome of dogmatically correct doggy mentality.

With some notable exceptions (see Shakespeare, below), the dog has been treated with respect and honor in Western literature. That probably has something to do with the fact that literature up until relatively recently has been dominated by men rather than women.

Men always get sentimental about the appurtenances of their vocations or their avocations.

Knights named their swords, their lances, their steeds, their faithful hounds. True, the naming lacked variety and inspiration, leaning heavily on commonplaces like "Betsy," "Nell," or "Bill." Nevertheless, this affection embraced dogs, who in the writing of men nearly always came off more courageous, more loyal, and smarter than they actually were.

Dante's *Inferno* is an exception. It includes a dog with three heads named Cerberus, stolen from Greek mythology and assigned as a symbol of gluttony. (Everything in the *Inferno* has three of something or other. If for some reason you don't care for the number three, don't read the book, which, by the way, is one of three books in Dante's *Divine Comedy*.) The symbolism is appropriate because dogs don't know when to quit eating. Never take a dog to a smorgasbord. It is not a pretty picture. Moreover, even with two extra heads, Cerberus is still a dumb dog. It is a curious case of one plus two adding up to nothing at all.

Writers in the middle ages devoted much time to descriptions of hunting, which they all regarded as a fine thing. (This was before Disney came along with all that *Bambi* nonsense and gave hunting a bad reputation.) Since hounds were major contributors to a hunt, they were rewarded with a fair share of any game that was

run down. Thus was initiated the very first profit-sharing plan (see Q and A, below).

But hunting was never about just getting
meat, and the dogs always knew that. And the
men knew it, as well, but they didn't tell their
wives about it. Wives and cats, especially after
the coming of agriculture, came to think such
things are silly: the ceremonious hunt, the risk-
taking, the self-testing. Where they are con-
cerned it's like bull-fighting or mountain climb-
ing and all those other dangerous games men
play, danger being one of the most important
components of the game. They would as soon
tend to breaking glass ceilings, thank you. If
dogs and men want to kill themselves playing
their little games, fine.

Dogs get the point about hunting, of course, that it is a quasi-religious occasion for men and dogs to get together and play poker and drink before they go out to kill Bambi's mother. That is why, although unlettered in the traditional sense, dogs are fond of literature, while cats are more partial to trashy popular romance novels.

The great English masterpiece *Sir Gawain and the Green Knight*, written by an anonymous poet when the language and the literature was in its infancy, features hunting prominently, along with some bedroom scenes that even cats might like. Gawain, headed for a confrontation with the Green Knight, takes respite from his journey with a stay at the castle of a friendly lord and an even friendlier lady. The lord of the castle proposes that they go out to hunt, but Gawain declines, claiming exhaustion.

While the lord is out hunting, his wife stays home and flirts with Gawain. Being the first Boy Scout, Gawain gently rebuffs her attentions, but allows her only one sweet kiss.

The lord of the castle takes his dogs out and first pursues the deer. The second day he goes after the boar, and the third day, the fox. Gawain, meanwhile, emulates the characteristics of each of those animals as he is pursued by the lord's wife, being at first elusive like the deer, then defensive like the boar, and finally cunning like the fox. Each day he receives a kiss, but on the third day, the lady throws her garter belt into the bargain.

Each day the lord comes back from the hunt and offers to exchange what he has garnered during the day for what Gawain has received. So Gawain accepts the deer and the boar and the fox, and gives the lord a kiss each day. However, he holds out on the garter belt, thinking the lord might take it the wrong way. Besides, he'd like to see what he looks like in the thing.

To make the story short, the lord turns out to be the Green Knight, and he spares Gawain from beheading only because Gawain has been most-ly honest, but he gives Gawain a nick on the neck for holding out on the garter belt, which the Green Knight wanted to try on for himself.

Thus was initiated the Royal Order of the Garter Belt, and the motto: *Honi soit qui mal y pense*, which means "I know wearing this thing looks bad, but I can explain."

Dogs, predictably, interpret the allegory in their own way. Gawain was foolish, they believe, with this lady crawling all over him, to come away with only a few kisses and an undergarment. He could have been out hunting and had some *real* run.

There are too many instances of dogs in English literature to recount them all. Chaucer gives

**Cerberus, proof that three heads are not
better than one.**

dogs to his Prioress, for example, and makes her
out a great dog lover. And of course, his Monk is
a hunter completely equipped with greyhounds.
Robinson Crusoe had a dog as a sidekick
(Thursday, we think its name was) before he had
Friday.

It was in American Literature that the dog
came into his own, however. In America, man
got a chance to start over and do it right, leaving

European civilization behind and striking out into the wilderness. Hunting once again was undertaken as a practical enterprise, and dogs, as partners in that enterprise, were once again elevated to a high eminence.

The folklore of America is rife with stories of dogs. For instance, there is the oft-repeated story of the "split dog," who while out hunting ran into a wire fence and was cut completely in two. His master patched the two halves back together again, but being in a hurry, got one half on upside down. It was thought at first that the dog was ruined for hunting, but soon it was discovered that the dog could make better time than before. When he got tired of running on two legs, he just flipped over and ran on the other two.

Another tale recounts the story of one of the fastest dogs ever, the Sooner Hound, who was speedy enough to race freight trains. When his master got a job as engineer on the Cannonball, everyone thought the dog may have met its match. The Cannonball was driven at top speed, and the dog seemed to be flagging. He was discovered, however, scooting up and down beside the speeding train on three legs, with his remaining leg lifted in a desperate attempt to cool off the overheated journal boxes.

Mark Twain tells the story of Jim Smiley's bull-pup in "The Jumping Frog of Calaveras County."

The bull-pup was a fighting dog whose strategy was to chomp onto a rear leg and hold on for dear life. The only match the dog lost was when he was pitted against a dog with no hind legs. After that he was a broken dog, wandered away, lay down and died.

Thomas Bangs Thorpe wrote one of the greatest tributes to a dog in "The Big Bear of Arkansas." The dog's name was Bowieknife:

> ". . . why the fellow thinks that the world is full of bear, he finds them so easy. It's lucky he don't talk as well as think; for with his natural modesty, if he should suddenly learn how much he is acknowledged to be ahead of all other dogs in the universe, he would be astonished to death in two minutes. Strangers, that dog know a bear's way as well as a horse-jockey knows a woman's: he always barks at the right time, bites at the exact place, and whips without getting a scratch. I never could tell whether he was made expressly to hunt bear, or whether bear was made expressly for him to hunt; any way, I believe they were ordained to go together naturally as Squire Jones says a man and woman is, when he moralizes in marrying a couple. In fact, Jones once said, said he, 'Marriage according to law is a civil contract of divine origin; it's common to all countries as well as Arkansaw, and people take to it as naturally as Jim Doggett's Bowieknife takes to bear.'" (T.B. Thorpe, "The Big Bear of Arkansas," in Walter Blair, *Native American Humor*, Chandler Pub. Co., San Francisco, p. 340)

Bowieknife is the obvious precursor of the dog in Faulkner's story, *The Bear.*

Dogs admire the writing of William Faulkner, mostly on the basis of *The Bear.* The first part of the story grips them especially, since it is about hunting and features dogs in key, even heroic roles.

They have greater difficulty with the second part, which is mostly about people and is written in long clauses and phrases that pile up like snowdrifts on Dakota barrens. Having been drilled in diagramming sentences in the fifth grade, Plutonians reflexively sniff out nouns and verbs and adverb clauses and participles and prepositional phrases and all the rest and expect the architecture to be as neat and tidy as that of a wood frame house. In Faulkner they find plenty of participles and a plethora of colons and semicolons, but a mighty paucity of main clauses and periods, along with an architecture that most resembles a Minoan maze. Here is represented the true danger of a little learning: it can blind the soul to the truth that lies beyond superficial form. Cats aren't as fussy about grammar, naturally, but they moan over "big words."

Some have discovered that the second part of the work makes a lot more sense when it is read as it was written, in a slightly inebriated condition. After a few shots, its true profundity emerges. The trouble with that school of literary

criticism, of course, is that one wakes up in the morning with a splitting headache and a foul breath to find that the clarity of the vision achieved the night before has fled.

Overall, however, dogs are willing to put up with Faulkner's stylistic peculiarities in order to relish the richness of his characters and his affinity for canine nobility. As one Dalmatian put it, "Old Bill knows his dogs, even if he is shy a few dots."

The Bear is told from the perspective of a boy, Ike McCaslin, and recounts the pursuit of a bear of mythological proportions who has earned the name of Ben and the courage of a blue dog named Lion. (Will you cats in the back settle down, please? A great author can give a dog an emblematic cat name if he wants to.) It is set in the 19th Century in the hills and swamps of Faulkner's Yokanapogotawpawpawpha County, a place renowned for its many syllables. This county occupies the Mississippi River drainage from the Gulf of Mexico to just north of Winnipeg and therefore requires numerous words to describe.

Some literary dogs see the work as an amalgamation of *The Adventures of Huckleberry Finn* and *Moby Dick*, with Huck in the role of Ishmael. Most, however, are pleased to read it as the ultimate expression of what a dog and a man have in common besides fleas.

One thing that pleases dog readers about *The Bear* is that it is filled with smells. Faulkner has, among other virtues, one of the best noses in literature, and one can't read this story without being aware of its noisome, even clamorous nature. At some points, as in the description of Boon Hogganbeck's sty, the odors become downright deafening. Dogs like that.

Boon is a simple-minded quarter-blood Indian who takes one look at Lion and falls in love.

Therefore, among other things, *The Bear* is a love story and appeals mightily to both dogs and men who understand such things as the result of at one time being puppies and boys and later on being hunters together and eventually coming to smell the same.

Men learn a lot about life from the dogs they love, and the story is about that, as well. There are abiding verities that antedate civilization and will survive it: that is Faulkner's message, at least in part, and Mark Twain's and Herman Melville's too. Civilized man got beached on the shoals of the American wilderness, shipwrecked like Crusoe, and was forced to start all over to think what exactly he was. All that European baloney about how man differs from the animals, used in defense of the most inhumane atrocities, didn't wash for the man with his back to the shore, facing the wild forests and the American deserts. He had to learn anew, and he took his lessons from the Indians and from animals, and especially from the dogs who cowered beside him.

Dog's delight in the variety of Plutonian personalities represented in *The Bear*. This is something that dogs understand that humans don't, unless they have had many dogs around them at the same time, have raised them from pups, say, or have hunted behind them. There are as many personalities represented in a pack of hounds as at a New York cocktail party. Some dogs are jealous and can't stand anybody showing attention to any other animal. Others are kindly and self-effacing. Some are brave; some are cowards. Some are dignified; some are clowns. And curiously, each is not only a type, but unique, as well, so that men who run numbers of dogs recognize them not only by their markings but also by their characters.

Like most good writers, Faulkner gives identifiable characteristics even to dogs in minor roles. For example there is the nameless bitch who loses part of an ear to Ben's savage claws and is tended to by the wise old Indian guide, Sam Fathers:

> "Just like a man," Sam said. "Just like folks. Put off as long as she could having to be brave, knowing all the time that sooner or later she would have to be brave once so she could keep on calling herself a dog, and knowing beforehand what was going to happen when she done it." (*The Portable Faulker,* ed. Mcalcom Cowley, New York: The Viking Press, 1966, p. 204)

The bitch who wades in and faces certain mutilation "so she could keep on calling herself a dog" is as redolent of the psychology of courage as Stephen Crane's great study of the subject in human terms. Dogs give her five stars.

Another dog who receives Plutonian plaudits is the feisty little ratter, called a "fyce," whose bravery exceeds its good sense. It attacks the

Dogs go to confession

raging bear like sparrow harassing a hawk and
has to be rescued from total destruction by the
boy. Dogs just have to smile when they read
about the fyce: they've known dogs who are just
that way.

Cats go the complaint department.

They know what Sam Fathers means, as well, when he says that being scared is natural and can't be helped, but that one must avoid being afraid. A coward gives in to his fear; courage lies in facing up to it. What is called for in the pursuit of old Ben is a dog strong, courageous, and resolute, and the climax of the hunt waits on the appearance of such a worthy: Lion. (Oh, will you cats shut up back there.)

Lion, who is part airedale and nine parts something else, hellhound or hound of heaven, puts humans to shame: "I ain't fit to sleep with him," Boon says. (*The Portable Faulkner, 228*) The dog had jumped the great bear and held it at bay, waiting for someone to come and kill it, but Boon had shot five times and had missed every time, accounting for why the South lost the Civil War.

If you've read *Moby Dick*, you have some idea what the final confrontation is going to be like. It is a confrontation with the mystery that is alien to us and threatening, the mystery that is as familiar to us as a noble dog, and the mystery inside us that preceded civilization and ownership and the curse of slavery and which will endure and prevail. Dogs get it immediately and instinctively. Cats, again, have trouble with the vocabulary, being too lazy to crack a dictionary.

Maybe you have to be an Epicurean atomist to get it at all, or even a part of it, but when dogs come across the following passage as they stagger drunkenly through the second part of the story, they underline it and underline it again and put an X in the margin to mark it and circle the X and put an exclamation point after the circle:

> . . . he had not stopped, he had only
> paused, quitting the knoll which was no
> abode of the dead because there was no
> death, not Lion and not Sam: not held fast in
> earth but free in earth and not in earth but of
> earth, myriad yet undiffused of every myriad
> part, leaf and twig and particle, air and sun
> and rain and day and night, acorn oak and
> leaf and acorn again, dark and dawn and
> dark and dawn again in their immutable pro-
> gression and, being myriad, one . . . (*The
> Portable Faulkner*, 317-318)

As for you cats, stop asking what "myriad" means. Look it up.

Saturnians, who know nothing about bears (except that they are spoilsports inhabiting Wall Street) and who hunt nothing more ferocious than a field mouse or a sparrow, have a hard time relating to Faulkner. They have an easier time of it with Ernest Hemingway. He wrote short sentences and used words that did not force cats to guess at their meanings. Another thing in Hemingway's favor, of course, is that he was a cat man who bred a six-toed variety. How can you not love a chap who sees how useful the extra traction might be for a cat?

Cats have heard the rumors about Hemingway shooting at cats when he was in Africa, but they are sure that if he did, he must have had a good reason. Of course, they would forgive any writer who could recount that beautiful bit about the leopard frozen in the high, icy reaches of Kilimanjaro and who showed such attentiveness to the feline species as he did in the short story "A Cat in the Rain," where a Saturnian has a featured and sympathetic role in words of one syllable.

Hemingway was a hunter, perhaps, but of that civilized Northern species that eschews the barbarity of running a pack of dogs through the swamps. He wrote more about fishing than hunting, and cats have respect for someone who brings home the tuna. So if they can't get hold of a steamy romance novel, cats will settle for Ernest. He could write Faulkner under the table any day, *they* think.

Cats are plentiful in literature and folklore, although not quite as plentiful as are dogs, perhaps. Mark Twain recounts the sad tale of the Quartzite Cat who lost his taste for quartzite mining after being blown sky-high in a mining accident. And lumbermen like to describe the antics of the Splinter Cat, who dive-bombs trees indescriminately in search of honey. Ambrose Bierce, who seemed to dislike cats, dogs, and humans with becoming disinterest, describes the terrible implosion that resulted as the result of the enmity between the patrons of a purveyor of cat-meat and the ghostly subjects of her husband, a dead-dog deoderizer.

But cats reserve their highest accolades for a surprising member of the literary pantheon: T.S.

Eliot. Here is a writer who *loves* cats, and is not afraid of admitting it. In "The Waste Land," a poem famous for its footnotes, he wrote the line most quoted by Saturnians: "Oh keep the dog far hence that's friend to man."

The work that cements Eliot's reputation in the hearts of cats, however, is *Old Possum's Book of Cats*. Tabby finds it charming that a major poet would squander his talents on an entire book devoted to the feline denomination. True, it is a short book, but every page of it weeps with the poet's dedication to his chosen deities.

And just when Saturnians thought that they couldn't do any better, along came *Cats,* the Andrew Lloyd Weber musical based on Eliot's book. As dancers and musicians themselves, and of the peculiar nature that allows them to hum every song of every musical ever written, cats everywhere stood tiptoe and arched their backs in saluting what they recognized as the longest running production on Broadway featuring whiskers and long tails. And when dogs get snooty about the preponderance of literature with a canine aroma, cats smile and ask how many musicals have been written about dogs. Hint: you don't need six toes to add them up. So there.

CATS AND DOGS IN SHAKESPEARE

> SPEED: But tell me true, will't be a match?
> LAUNCE: Ask my dog: if he say ay, it will! if he say no, it will; if he shake his tail and say nothing, it will.
> — *The Two Gentlemen of Verona: Act II, Scene v*

Because of Shakespeare's superior intelligence and his ability to use language for something other than purring or barking, scholars believe that he may have come, not from Mars, Venus, Saturn, or Pluto, but from another planet entirely, perhaps even from a Galaxy Far, Far Away.

A recent study of his works, conducted by a doctoral candidate desperate to pluck yet another dissertation topic from the scraps remaining after decades of relentless over-examination, concludes that Shakespeare was — and here I must ask any dogs reading this to sit down and brace themselves — a cat lover.

The thesis, as usual, is overstated. The bard actually was not so much a lover of cats as tolerant of cats. Fortunately for cats, that amounts to the same thing. For dogs he seems to have harbored some kind of grudge. While dogs may take solace in the fact that references to them in Shakespeare's canon outnumbers references to

Kitty helps Shakespeare write Macbeth.

cats three to one, the sad truth is that the word "dog" is used in his writing for the most part the way cats use it, as a swear word.

The reason given for Shakespeare's antipathy toward dogs is an *ad hominem* one, or perhaps *ad caninem*. Obviously, says the study, he was once bitten by a mad dog, perhaps while growing up in Bottles by Avon. Evidence in his work is bountiful. A small example is this passage:

O Buckingham, take heed of yonder dog!
Look, when he fawns, he bites; and when he
    bites,
His venom tooth will rankle to the death:
Have not to do with him, beware of him;
Sin, death, and hell have set their marks on
    him,
And all their ministers attend on him.
— *King Richard III: Act I, Scene iii*

Gee, the average dog will whine, that seems a little unfair, doesn't it, to judge all dogs by the aberrant behavior of one? Well, it may be unfair, but Shakespeare was writing before the advent of political correctness, and he lets dogs have it with both barrels:

From forth the kennel of thy womb hath
    crept
A hell-hound that doth hunt us all to death:
That dog, that had his teeth before his eyes,
To worry lambs and lap their gentle blood,
That foul defacer of God's handiwork,
That excellent grand tyrant of the earth,
That reigns in galled eyes of weeping souls,
Thy womb let loose, to chase us to our
    graves.
O upright, just, and true-disposing God,
How do I thank thee, that this carnal cur
Preys on the issue of his mother's body,
And makes her pew-fellow with others'
    moan!
— *King Richard III: Act IV, Scene iv*

In the interest of fairness, it must be allowed that the word "cat" is sometimes used by Shakespeare as an epithet, as well. In his poem *Lu-*

crece, which is read once every five years by a Shakespearean scholar in Patagonia, one finds the following phrase: "foul night-waking cat." Unhappily, nobody knows exactly what that means or whether it is really an unfavorable expression or not.

Cats have taken a vote and have overwhelmingly approved the interpretation that the adjective "foul" applies not to the noun "cat" but to the noun "night," while the adjective "waking," which has nothing but favorable connotations, is applied to the noun "cat." On the bright side, nobody really cares very much about this issue except the Shakespearean scholar in Patagonia.

Less ambiguous, perhaps, are these words by Bertram in Act IV, Scene iii, of *Alls Well That Ends Well*: "I could endure any thing before but a cat, and now he's a cat to me." And Lysander, in Act III, Scene ii of *A Midsummer Night's Dream* is equally clear: "Hang off, thou cat, thou burr!/vile thing,let loose, / Or I will shake thee from me like a serpent!"

For every condemnation of Saturnian kind, however, one might find in the poet's work kinder, gentler references: "a harmless necessary cat," for example, is found in *The Merchant of Venice*, Act IV, Scene i. About this phrase there is little dispute, and cats, especially, are in unanimous agreement that both the adjective "harmless" and the adjective "necessary" apply most fittingly to the noun "cat."

They do have some difficulty, however, with the adage "care killed a cat," found in Act V, Scene i of *Much Ado About Nothing*. The saw makes no sense, cats protest. Cats flourish on care, cannot get enough of it, want it, desire it, long for it, even if they prefer to be ingrateful for it when it is given. Besides, what's so bad about dying and going to Tuna?

Of considerable consolation to the much abused dogs is the fact that they actually appeared on stage at Shakespeare's Globe Theater (or Theatre, as it is spelled by drama majors). It is true that female dogs had to be played by male dogs, since at the time acting was held in such low repute that even promiscuous bitches felt the trade beneath them, but dogs did have roles, if not lines.

The most notable example is the central position taken by a dog in *Two Gentlemen of Verona*. In that play, a servant by the name of Launce appears not once, but twice with his dog in tow, and in both instances launches into long and noteworthy, albeit one-sided, dialogue with the beast. The first sample comes from Act II, Scene iii:

> I think Crab, my dog, be the sourest-natured
> dog that lives: my mother weeping, my fa-

Panter in MacBeth, assaying the crucial role of "Spot."

ther wailing, my sister crying, our maid howling, our cat wringing her hands, and all our house in a great perplexity, yet did not this cruel-hearted cur shed one tear: he is a stone, a very pebble stone, and has no more pity in him than a dog: a Jew would have wept to have seen our parting; why, my grandam, having no eyes, look you, wept herself blind at my parting.

Nay, I'll show you the manner of it. This shoe
is my father: no, this left shoe is my father:
no, no, this left shoe is my mother: nay,
that cannot be so neither: yes, it is so, it is
so, it hath the worser sole. This shoe, with
the hole in it, is my mother, and this my father; a vengeance on't! there 'tis: now, sit,
this staff is my sister, for, look you, she is
as white as a lily and as small as a wand:
this hat is Nan, our maid:

I am the dog: no, the dog is himself, and I am
the dog--Oh! the dog is me, and I am my-
self; ay, so, so.
Now come I to my father; Father, your
blessing: now should not the shoe speak a
word for weeping: now should I kiss my father; well, he weeps on.
Now come I to my mother: O, that she could
speak now like a wood woman! Well, I kiss
her; why, there 'tis; here's my mother's
breath up and down. Now come I to my
sister; mark the moan she makes.

Now the dog all this while sheds not a tear
nor speaks a word; but see how I lay the
dust with my tears.

The drama continues in Act IV, Scene iv:

When a man's servant shall play the cur with
him, look you, it goes hard: one that I
brought up of a puppy; one that I saved
from drowning, when three or four of his
blind brothers and sisters went to it.

I have taught him, even as one would say
precisely, 'thus I would teach a dog.' I was
sent to deliver him as a present to Mistress
Silvia from my master; and I came no
sooner into the dining-chamber but he
steps me to her trencher and steals her
capon's leg: O, 'tis a foul thing when a cur
cannot keep himself in all companies!

I would have, as one should say, one that
takes upon him to be a dog indeed, to be,
as it were, a dog at all things.

If I had not had more wit than he, to take a
fault upon me that he did, I think verily he
had been hanged for't; sure as I live, he
had suffered for't; you shall judge.   He
thrusts me himself into the company of
three or four gentlemanlike dogs under
the duke's table: he had not been there--
bless the mark!--a pissing while, but all the
chamber smelt him.

'Out with the dog!' says one: 'What cur is
that?' says another: 'Whip him out' says
the third: 'Hang him up' says the duke. I,
having been acquainted with the smell before, knew it was Crab, and goes me to the
fellow that whips the dogs: 'Friend,' quoth
I, 'you mean to whip the dog?' 'Ay, marry,
do I,' quoth he. 'You do him the more
wrong,' quoth I; ''twas I did the thing you
wot of.' He makes me no more ado, but
whips me out of the chamber.

How many masters would do this for his servant? Nay, I'll be sworn, I have sat in the
stocks for puddings he hath stolen, otherwise he had been executed; I have stood

Sir Herbert of York, in the role of "Crab," striking a favorite pose.

on the pillory for geese he hath killed, otherwise he had suffered for't.

Thou thinkest not of this now. Nay, I remember the trick you served me when I took my leave of Madam Silvia: did not I bid

> thee still mark me and do as I do? when
> didst thou see me heave up my leg and
> make water against a gentlewoman's far-
> thingale? didst thou ever see me do such a
> trick?

The original portrayer of Launce's Dog, whose name was Sir Herbert of York, was knighted in his sunset years specifically for this, er, water-shed performance.

Dogs adore these scenes, even if the dog character is cast in a somewhat unfavorable light, because it demonstrates the kind of loyalty they would like to get from their masters and so seldom receive. Dog's everywhere give this play a standing ovation, erect on three feet while raising the right hindquarters in what has become renowned as "Sir Herbert's salute."

QUESTIONS AND ANSWERS
ABOUT DOGS AND CATS

What is the most expensive breed of dog?

The pit bull. It costs an arm and a leg.

Why does a dog stick its head out a car window?

There are four major theories: 1. He is fantasizing that he can fly like a cat. 2. He is drying his hair. 3. He is sniffing a Porsche. 4. He is hitting on the poodle in the next lane.

Are there any dog or cat addicts?

Catnip is regarded as a "recreational drug" by most cats, but some warn it can lead to the "hard stuff." By "hard stuff" is meant floral arrangements. As for dogs, just two words: cat turds.

Is it true that St. Francis loved all animals?

Yes, although he never met a pekinese.

What's wrong with a pekinese?

That is a much-pondered question. Here is a ponderous answer: A pekinese, unlike many other dogs, has never taken up honest labor. Unable to do anything really useful, it became a critic. It offers its opinion frequently and loudly, becoming foremost among yap dogs. It is, furthermore, dishonest in its criticism, preferring its own cleverness of expression for a reasoned appraisal. As a result, it has been enormously popular among the undiscerning.

How do you like the poodle?

Grilled, with a side of fries.

Do people really eat dogs and cats?

Not that they will admit. It's always somebody else who did that, as is also the case with cannibalism. But how else do you account for the juicy Mexican hairless? Or for those cat whiskers that kept showing up in meat pies in London in the 19th Century?

How do they taste?

Dogs, like venison. Cats, like tuna. If somebody says they taste like chicken, he is lying, although cats in London in the 19th Century were sometimes know as "Chicken of the Streets."

Come on, stop gagging. You eat cows, pigs, even turkeys. Grow up.

In related news, the American Vegetarian Society is seeking new members.

Naughty Doggies go to obedience shool.

Naughty kitties go into therapy.

What is the difference between a pointer and a setter?

While both are bird dogs, the pointer is in the accusative case. A setter is another case entirely. Incidentally, a setter does not violate dog grammar (see above) as many believe. A setter does not *sit* at all, but rather crouches in the weeds, immobile, when it has spotted game. "To set" in this instance, means "to become rigid," like a bowl of gelatin hardening in the refrigerator. And like a bowl of gelatin, the setter is allowed to quiver in excitement. For some reason males make better pointers; females make better setters. Investigation into this curious fact is continuing at this writing.

What do you get when you cross a pointer with a setter?

A poinsetter. It would make an excellent Christmas gift for people who don't have a green thumb.

However, crossbreeding bird dogs is strictly forbidden by the very strong bird-dog union, which insists on separation of job descriptions. A pointer can't set. A setter can't point. A springer can't retrieve. A retriever can't spring, point, or set. These regulations make it difficult for hunters, who must take four dogs along to get one lousy pheasant. Some hunters have become so flustered trying to handle four dogs that they've completely forgotten to bring along their guns.

There is, nevertheless, a flourishing black market in crossbreeds: poinsetters, sprinters, sprintrievers, and the all around bird dog, the sprointsetriever.

What do you get when you cross a bird-dog picket line with a scab?

An Owy.

Does a boxer actually box?

Boxing is a lost art. There are only sluggers and wrestlers. It is curious, by the way, that a box is cubic, a ring is round, but a boxing ring is square. Boxing promoters sometimes have cylindrical hair, but that is getting into another dimension entirely. What I'd really like to know is what any of this has to do with dogs.

Why are golden retrievers so nice?

They can't help themselves. Just as some dogs are "born to be wild," golden retrievers are bred to be nice. In the field one must use a gentle tone: "Please go fetch the duck." After delivering their bird, they expect only a simple "thank you," to which they will reply, "You're very welcome." Their politeness sometimes reaches oppressive proportions. We do not live in a polite age, so golden retrievers seem aberrant. Phrases like "thank you," "if you don't mind," "after you," and "pass the crackers, please," so often communicated by the breed, take up valuable time that we could be using to surf the net.

Some owners of golden retrievers attempt to break their pets of the habit of politeness by confining them for several days in a small pen along with a doberman pinscher and a pit bull. One such owner opened the pen after three days to find both the doberman and the pit bull dead, the retriever alive and wagging its tail in a non-assertive manner. At first the owner thought that the other two dogs had killed each other, but on closer examination he found that neither of the dead dogs had a mark on it. They had died of overweening niceness.

How many dogs does it take to change a light bulb.?

Five. Union rules.

How many cats does it take to change a light bulb?

None. Cats don't do bulbs.

How do you draw a cat?

Get drunk. Then try to draw a dog.

Are dogs and cats religious?

Dogs are religious. Cats are a religion. Curiously, dogs worship not cats, but men, with whom they share the humble conviction that human beings were created in God's image.

Women, on the other hand, do worship cats. Men worship women. It is all something like a food chain.

Do dogs and cats go to heaven?

Heaven's gate, it turns out, has much in common with the kitchen door. Dogs with muddy paws are turned away. Cats are admitted because even St. Peter can't stand their bawling to be let in. Since there is nothing to do in heaven, it suits cats perfectly. After a few centuries, dogs get to thinking it might be more fun in the Other Place.

Do dogs and cats have a sense of humor?

Dogs can get a joke, but cats can't, having no sense of humor at all. True, dog jokes are often crude and even offensive to sensitive ears. Consequently, they are told only in small unmixed groups. Typical feeble dog joke: "Did you hear the one about the guy who called his dog 'Kitty' and fed it tuna? Whenever the dog peed on the floor, the guy told his wife, 'Kitty did it,' and kicked the cat. One day the cat peed on the floor and the guy told his wife, 'Kitty did it,' and she kicked the dog. 'Why did you kick the dog?' the guy asked. And she said, 'What dog?'"

Typical cat response: "Silly."

What do dogs have against mailmen?

Dogs are offended by what they perceive to be an uneven playing field. According to signs pinned up in post offices everywhere, "It is a federal offense to assault a postal employee." Yet kicking a dog is not even a misdemeanor in most localities. Dogs are lobbying to make it a federal offense punishable by life imprisonment to assault a dog. What they're really afraid of is that a disgruntled postal employee may go berserk and head for a kennel carrying an Uzi. It could happen.

What are the hardest working dogs?

Members of dog teams. Pulling a dog sled is really hard work, especially if you happen to get a flat. The team could start pulling to the right and you could just keep going around the pole. That's why most drivers carry at least two spares: one husky and one malamute, just in case the husky goes flat, too.

How do dog sled drivers get their teams to work so hard?

Some drivers try profit-sharing, which works pretty well until the dogs find out how much of a snowshoe rabbit they get when it's split eighteen ways. Others make up half their teams in interns who work hard for nothing but the experience and a reference that will look good on a

resumé. Still others hire only half-time dogs at a quarter of the salary. This last strategy works best; the dogs have to have at least two jobs to make a living, but at least they're working. It's a good thing men aren't as dumb as dogs.

What is the best job for a dog?

A seeing-eye dog has the best occupation because he gets to exercise his wit on the job. He can stop suddenly on the sidewalk and carefully maneuver around an imaginary open manhole, and the guy he's leading will say, "Good dog," and give him a pig's ear. Seeing-eye dogs get a big kick out of that one. Or he can stop halfway across a street and make a turn and lead the guy up the center line and at the next corner go on across the street as though everything was normal. The guy he's leading will say, "Good dog," and give him a pig's ear. That's a pretty good one, too, for seeing-eye dogs.

Once in a while, however, a joke will backfire. One dog was leading a guy through the park when he stopped and backed up. The guy sat down, thinking he was by a park bench, and fell flat. Then the guy stood up and said , "Bad dog," and gave the dog a kick. And the dog said, "Gee, some people are as bad as cats. They have no sense of humor."

What happens when a seeing-eye dog gets cataracts?

He gets another seeing-eye dog. If this happens often enough, the blind guy can ride in a sled.

Why are dogs afraid of vacuum cleaners?

That is another instinct that dogs and men share. To a dog, a vacuum cleaner looks like a giant cat going "CAAHT" very loudly. To a man, it looks like work.

There's one breed, Lopsa Asso, I think it's called. How exactly is it pronounced and what does it mean?

"Lopsa Asso"? I think you must mean what some call Lotsa Alpo, the Tibetan breed that used to guard very small temples against attacks by very small cats. In Tibetan the name is spelled "Lhasa" (which follows the Tibetan spelling rule of A-before-H-except-after-L)

"Apso" (which does not), which is not to be confused with the Appa Loosa and is pronounced either "LAYS-ah-APE-so" or "LASS-ee-AP-soo" or "LAH-sah-AHP-see" or (in southern Tibet only) "LOSS-uh-OHP-suh, Y'ALL." The name means literally "Furball Walking.," and its Latin designation is *Plutonus Yapsalottus Adeste Fidelis Opera Citado,* or in plain English, "Fido." On a more figurative level it means "the end of civilization as we know it." On a personal note, I hope you appreciate the hours of scholarly research that went into this answer and I hope you're satisfied, you rascal you.

How do you train a police dog?

You teach it to say "Freeze!" in a commanding voice.

Is that all there is to it?

No, you also have to get it to memorize a prisoner's Miranda rights and not just read it off a card, which looks bad on television.

Do dogs make good witnesses?

The O.J. case offers a good example. A dog is the only witness who had the opportunity to see what actually happened, and it is apparently not telling all it knows. It may be that it has taken note of the meteoric celebrity of the human witnesses who spoke out, like Kato What's-his-name, or perhaps, as some insiders suspect, he is holding out for a better deal on book rights. One thing I'm sure of, we haven't heard the last of this one yet.

IN CONCLUSION

By now you get the idea. Dogs are way different from cats, and only this book tells you just how different and what you can do about it. If you enjoyed what you read here, be sure to look for forthcoming volumes by the same author, *The Feline Prophecy* or *Cats Do Too Have Souls, Chicken Soup for Your Puppy, Chicken Soup for Your Kitty,* and *Cats Are From Saturn — Dogs Are From Pluto II: What to Do When Your Pets Turn on You And Demand a Share of the Royalties.*

And in the how-to field, look for *How to Make Big Bucks by Telling People What They Already Know,* and *If You Think This is Good, I've Got a Property in the Swamps of Brazil You Should See.*

We cherish our readers, especially if they paid cash, and in the interest of kissing up to them, we invite them to write with comments and suggestions. Address your letters of praise and donations (cashier's check or money order, please) to the author in care of the publisher. Address corrections, complaints, and nasty slurs to Newt Gingrich, in care of the Congress of the United States, Washington, D.C.